PLATFORM PAPERS

QUARTERLY ESSAYS ON THE PERFORMING ARTS FROM CURRENCY HOUSE

No. 61
November 2019

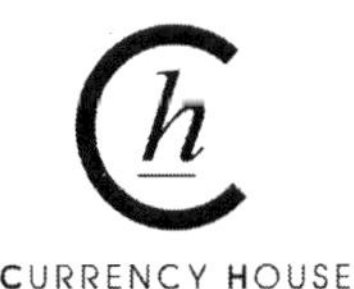

Platform Papers Partners

We acknowledge with gratitude our Partners in continuing support of Platform Papers and its mission to widen understanding of performing arts practice and encourage change when it is needed:

Neil Armfield, AO
Anita Luca Belgiorno-Nettis Foundation
Jane Bridge
Katharine Brisbane, AM
Elizabeth Butcher, AM
Penny Chapman
Dr Peter Cooke, AM
Sally Crawford
Wesley Enoch
Ferrier Hodgson
Larry Galbraith
Wayne Harrison, AM
Campbell Hudson
Lindy Hume
Justice François Kunc
Dr Richard Letts, AM
Peter Lowry, OAM and Carolyn Lowry, OAM
David Marr
Helen O'Neil
Lesley Power
Professor William Purcell
Queensland Performing Arts Centre Trust
Geoffrey Rush, AC
Dr Merilyn Sleigh
Maisy Stapleton
Augusta Supple
Christopher Tooher
Caroline Verge
Queensland Performing Arts Trust
Rachel Ward, AM and Bryan Brown, AM
Kim Williams, AM

To them and to all subscribers and Friends of Currency House we extend our grateful thanks.

Platform Papers Readers' Forum

Readers' responses to our previous essays are posted on our website. Contributions to the conversation (250 to 2000 words) may be emailed to info@currencyhouse.org.au. The Editor welcomes opinion and criticism in the interest of healthy debate but reserves the right to monitor where necessary.

Platform Papers, quarterly essays on the performing arts, is published every February, May, August and November and is available through bookshops, by subscription and on line in paper or electronic version. For details see our website at www.currencyhouse.org.au.

Criticism, Performance and the Need for Conversation

ALISON CROGGON

ABOUT THE AUTHOR

ALISON CROGGON is a widely published novelist, poet, children's author, theatre writer and critic who lives in Melbourne. Her critical work has been published widely, including in *The Monthly*, *Overland*, *Australian Book Review*, Radio National and *The Guardian*. She was Melbourne theatre critic for *The Bulletin* 1989–92 and *The Australian* 2007–10. In 2004 she began writing Theatre Notes, which became essential reading for thoughtful theatregoers, and closed it in 2012. In 2009 Theatre Notes was the first digital critic to be named the Geraldine Pascall Critic of the Year. From 2013–15 she was national theatre critic for ABC Arts Online. In 2017, she co-founded the online critical website Witness (witnessperformance.com) with Robert Reid.

Her poetry has been widely published in journals both in Australia and overseas, and is included in many major Australian anthologies. Her most recent poetry collection is *New and Selected Poems 1991–2017* (Newport Street Books, 2017). Her poetry collections won the Anne Elder and Dame Mary Gilmore Prizes and have been shortlisted for the Victorian and NSW Premiers' Literary Awards.

She has written extensively for theatre and opera. *The Riders*, score by Iain Grandage, was named Choral/

Vocal Work of the Year in the 2015 Art Music Awards. The libretto for *Mayakovsky* (score by Michael Smetanin) was shortlisted for the 2015 Victorian Premier's Literary Awards Drama prize. In 2019 her play *My Dearworthy Darling* had its premiere at the Malthouse Theatre, Melbourne, in a co-production between Malthouse and the experimental theatre company, the Rabble.

Her novels include the bestselling epic fantasy series *The Books of Pellinor*; *Black Spring*, shortlisted for the NSW Premier's Literary Awards YA prize; and *The River and the Book*, winner of the Wilderness Society's Prize for Environmental Writing for Children; and shortlisted for the WA Premier's Award for YA fiction. Her first middle-grade novel, The Threads of Magic, will be released in the UK and Australia in 2020.

1. Some perspective

Human beings are chatty animals: we like to discuss the things we encounter. And we're also, for good and ill, animals that make things, a characteristic that expresses itself in the infinite variety of art-making we engage in. Consequently, for the past couple of millennia a good deal of human ingenuity has been expended on talking to each other about art.

The roots of arts criticism reach back into antiquity. European critical traditions begin with the writings of classical Greek and Roman philosophers; writings such as Aristotle's *Poetics* (335 BCE), Horace's *Ars Poetica* (c19 BCE) and Longinus's *On the Sublime* (100 BCE) form a bedrock that still informs Western thinking today.

Likewise, the Sanskrit text *Nātya Śāstra,* attributed to Bharata Muni (200 BCE-200 CE), is a treatise in 6,000 verses about the performing arts that was a formative influence on traditional dance and theatre making in India. In China, live performance is recorded as far back as the Shang Dynasty in 1600 BCE. In a passage in his *Records of the Grand Historian* (94 BCE), Sima Qian reports Confucius explaining the symbolism of the Dawu (Great Warrior) Dance: 'When they dance in two rows and lunge in all directions with their weapons, they are spreading the awe of his military might throughout the Central States.'

The tale of Australian performance criticism is a tiny twig of a much larger, multiple-branched narrative. Since Platform Papers is a series focussing upon the current health of the performing arts, I shall use the space to focus on performance criticism only, and even more particularly, on performance criticism in Australia in the wake of the digital revolution that has convulsed the publishing world since the turn of the millennium. But since many of the assumptions of this world remain profoundly shaped by European traditions of arts criticism, especially in the English-speaking world, it is worth stepping back and taking a lightning tour of its complicated past.

Modern arts criticism in the English-speaking world was born as a specifically colonial discourse in the chocolate and coffee houses of eighteenth-century London, where the wits and scribes of the day opined over 'stimulating beverages extracted from the labour of West Indian slaves'.[1]

According to the historian Matthew White, by the middle of the eighteenth century there were more than 550 coffee houses in London:

> *With their relaxed atmosphere and relative cheapness (at just one penny, the cost of a cup of coffee was usually included in the entry price of the establishment), many busy Londoners preferred the informal surroundings of the coffee house to the stuffiness of the royal court, legal chambers, offices and other places of professional business. Samuel*

> *Pepys noted extensively in his diary the usefulness of his visits to the coffee house, where he was able to pick up gossip, listen to debates or simply make useful trade connections. By 1664 Pepys was visiting his favourite coffee houses near London's Royal Exchange more than three times each week (and often twice a day), usually to meet his friends or colleagues by prior arrangement, or sometimes simply to overhear the stories of trade and politics told by strangers.*[2]

These coffee houses, exclusively patronised by men, became powerful centres of both commerce and culture. According to Matthew White, one coffee house opened by Edward Lloyd at the corner of Abchurch Lane in the 1680s grew in popularity with merchants and ship owners, who met there each day 'to gather intelligence of shipping, to auction cargoes and to report maritime disasters'. Lloyd's, of course, evolved into the vast agency dealing in maritime insurance brokerage that still flourishes in the City of London to this day.

Coffee houses were the seventeenth-century version of Twitter, purveying the currencies of scuttlebutt, gossip and economic, political and cultural intelligence, with an undertow of revolution. They were also instrumental in the development of modern publishing, books, newspapers and journals. Many newspapers supplied their wares free of charge, and even employed runners to spread 'news flashes' that couldn't wait for the press.

In 1688, James II banned the distribution of papers through coffee houses (aside from the official state paper the *London Gazette*) for fear of the insurrectionary ideas being circulated with them; but this didn't stop the founding of London's first daily newspaper, the *London Courant*, in 1702, and later Richard Steele's *Tatler* (1709) and Joseph Addison's *Spectator* (1711).

The growth of the publishing industry in the eighteenth century was explosive. By the end of it, there were 23 London newspapers and about 250 periodicals being published around Britain. The immediate result was a professionalisation of the writing classes: authors now found they could make a living from writing.

During the 1700s, this noisy discourse established itself as a tussle between the hacks of Grub Street—the noisome lane in Cripplegate inhabited by impoverished poets, low-end publishers and booksellers—and those who sought to bring order, propriety and elevation to the vulgar fray.

In *The Critic in the Modern World*, James Ley writes that Steele and Addison positioned themselves as defenders of propriety and good taste, 'advocating an ideal of gentility and cultivation'. They saw themselves as disseminators of the best ideas and promoters of healthy discussion. 'I have brought philosophy out of closets and libraries, schools and colleges', boasted Addison, 'to dwell in clubs and assemblies, at tea tables and in coffee houses.'[3]

Samuel Johnson began his career in Grub Street and was perhaps the first model of a critical man of letters, an arbiter of morality and taste. Like Steele and Addison, Johnson positioned himself above the vulgar press. In the *Idler* he described the 'news writer' as:

> *a man without virtue, who writes lies at home for his own profit. To these compositions is required neither genius nor knowledge, neither industry nor sprightliness, but contempt of shame and indifference to truth are absolutely necessary.*[4]

This struggle between the vulgar and the proper continued to shape critical discussion over the next few centuries. The cultural historian John Brewer observes:

> *Out of the publication emerged questions that were to vex authors, critics and the public for the next 200 years. Who were the public? How could one affect their taste? How could you discipline and control them in the world of a free press? And how were you to re-establish firm boundaries in a culture that seemed to be in flux?*[5]

These are questions—perhaps especially the notion of a need to 'discipline and control'—that haunt discussions about criticism still. It's not difficult to see echoes of Samuel Johnson's descriptions in contemporary anxieties about 'fake news', as assumptions of media authority—mostly, it must be said, promulgated by the media themselves—have come under pressure in the early twenty-first century as traditional media institutions have dissolved and reformed under the disruptions of the digital age.

But other contestations persist as well: questions of nationalism, and social ideas about race and gender. In his far-reaching cultural study, *Cities of the Dead,* Joseph Roach argues that the 'Human Invention' of theatre as a high-culture European, bourgeois art form occurred in the febrile atmosphere of money, gossip and performance that characterised the coffee houses of London.

Roach describes how the critical writing of the time helped to form the idea of the stage as a 'Mimic State', that reflects and legitimises the Sovereign state, with the body of the actor becoming an unstable medium between the dead and the living, the present and the past. The performance of culture, both on the stages of London and in the critical discourses around them, were instrumental to what he calls 'the production of human difference'—which is to say, the production of ideas of race, sexuality and gender that equipped and justified the emerging colonial imperialism.

He traces the beginning of the idea of a national stage to this time.

> *Beginning in the eighteenth century, a number of visionaries from George Farquhar to Friedrich Schiller turned to the concept of a national stage. More intensely than the solitary experience of readership, the provocative spectacle of the theatrical*

> *audience summons the idea of nationhood in the poignancy of its absence.*

As is the case now, the 1700s were a period of volatile change. The locus of political power—impelled in part by the colonial adventures of companies like Britain's East India Company—moved from aristocrats and the monarchy, to bourgeois bankers and insurers, leading both to the convulsions of the French Revolution in 1789 and the increasing economic and military dominance of the British Empire. In the early twenty-first century, we are in the midst of similar epoch-shaking shifts of power. Amid huge geopolitical shifts, we are witnessing the movement of political power from nation states into the hands of massive global corporations.

There are some interesting continuities—anxieties about authority, truth and the public, for example—that can be traced to four centuries ago. After all, some things haven't changed that much: Australia, founded in the first place to house the criminal classes of Georgian England, still recognises the British monarch as our head of state. And our post-invasion history, inflected through our critical discussions of all kinds, is informed by a hallucinatory dance of remembrance and forgetting that stems from being a settler colony.

Our critical culture is young compared to that of Europe, but until recently—drawing on models of authority derived from those London coffee houses—it's been mostly written by white men in a culture that is both explicitly and implicitly colonial. And contested notions of nationhood, freedom and human difference remain subliminally constitutive of many of the assumptions that underlie contemporary critical arguments in Australia.

The (beleaguered) role of the critic

Much of the debate and conflict that has dominated the past half century of Australian critical writing has been sparked by challenges to the hegemony of the colonial state, as represented both in bodies on stage and in the discourse around them. In the wake of the spectacular worldwide collapse of the business model of print journalism, there's been a lot of handwringing over the decline, or even the disappearance, of criticism. But very often, this isn't so much about the disappearance of criticism itself—cultural commentary being, if anything, more prevalent than it has ever been—as it is a lament for the decline of critical *authority*. Which is a rather different thing.

It's now commonplace to date the decline of the critic from the rise of the internet in the 1990s. But in fact a decline in the authority of the critic was noted long before. Criticism seems to be—along with that other dialogic art form, the theatre itself—constantly perceived to be in its death throes.

In a 1986 essay, the German poet Hans Magnus Enzensberger, cast a sardonic eye over the literary journalism of the time, and commented that 'there is only babble left'. 'Literature is free,' he adds, 'but it can neither legitimate nor call into question the constitution of the whole; it's allowed to do everything, but nothing depends on it anymore.'

> *... it seems that the appearance of the critic is related to the rise of bourgeois society, as if he had dominated this society for just as long as this society held on to the idea that the public discussion of cultural norms is something essential: that is, crudely put, from Boileau to Sartre, from Samuel Johnson to Edmund Wilson, from Lessing to Benjamin, from Belinsky to Shklovsky.*
>
> *What characterises these fabulous intellectual beasts? Legend has it, and it is confirmed by reading the works they left behind, that they were writers who wrote about the books of other writers. Further, these critics are said to have been independent people, who owed their significance solely to their work, not to an institution or an industry, at whose service they had placed themselves. Apparently, the essay was their preferred form, the journal their favoured medium. They are said to have known what they wanted—obstinate, uncomfortable spirits, looking to long-term results instead of quick turnover.*[6]

Enzensberger's polemic is a useful marker of the decline in social influence of the critics of the early twentieth century—intellectuals such as Edmund Wilson, Walter Benjamin, and Viktor Shklovsky—and their replacement by literary journalists and academics. He sees these as a self-perpetuating industry located in schools, universities and newspapers, their independence curtailed by their imbrication in the institutions that employ them. He calls them 'circulation agents' who belong 'overwhelmingly to the sphere of the free-market economy, [while the former] form the solid base of state culture.' Literary criticism, he concludes, has lost its spotlight as the expression of an age, buckling under late capitalism and the pressures of a pluralist consumerist economy.

He says it isn't as if writers are especially upset by the death of the critic: they keep on writing all the same. Literature has simply returned to its true scale, enjoyed by a literate minority of the interested:

> *This public uncoupled itself from the Punch and Judy show of the big media long ago. It forms its judgment independently of the chatter of the reviews and the talk shows, and the only kind of advertising it believes in is word of mouth, which is both free and beyond price.*

Enzensberger's essay is fascinating to read in 2019, not least because he speaks confidently of a 'public' that today seems both splintered and interestingly reconstituted by the world of social media. But it is also of note now because what feels under attack in the ongoing shocks of the digital age are the very same institutional critics and academics who replaced his 'fabulous intellectual beast', the independent critic.

It is this institutional authority that is often mourned and defended in newspaper columns. The institutional critics who have dominated public artistic discourse over recent decades are under extreme pressure themselves because of profound social shifts that were already under way in the 1980s, and which now have cumulatively built to the point of acute crisis.

In *Theatre Criticism: Changing Landscapes,* Duška Radosavljević traces the fortunes of art criticism through the twentieth century and takes Enzensberger's argument a step further. 'There seems to be a consensus [...] that the Age of Enlightenment originally gave birth to the figure of the critic,' she says. 'Ever since then, the critic occupied a position of authority as an arbiter of public taste and an 'expert' on a particular art form.'[7]

> *[U]ntil relatively recently, newspaper criticism and academic criticism still co-existed within interchangeable planes—[h]igh-profile critics of the mid-twentieth century were frequently university professors who wrote books and reviews for a non-academic audience. A significant rift occurred in the year 1968. The atmosphere of anti-authoritarianism, which spilled across the globe and led to demonstrations in various countries, coincided with the publication of Roland Barthes' essay, 'The Death of the Author' which argued against the critic seeing the work through the lens of his own experience on the grounds that the true value of the work lay in the reader's impression.*

> *Further development of left-leaning cultural theory deployed Marxist, feminist and poststructuralist perspectives in interpreting works of art in relation to their political context, uncovering their latent ideological content and the self-perpetuating workings of the dominant power structures—arguably taking academic criticism further away from the general public [...] This trend for interpretation reached a crisis in the early 2000s and a new way forward was needed.*[8]

These larger intellectual movements may seem abstruse in relation to the fate of theatre reviewing, which mostly occurred in newspapers and which, as Stella Gibbons once said of the journalistic style, can seem in comparison 'nasty, brutish and short'.[9] Theatre reviewing for the most part, and in Britain in particular, exists in a space somewhere between literature and journalism, with enduring characteristics that include 'bias in favour of actors and dramatic character, [...] suspicion of rules, [...] pragmatic reportage and [the] need [...] to persuade the reader that the theatre will do him good'.

In fact, the conventional form of a review in the English-speaking world has remained remarkably stable.

> *The reviewer should define his/her relationships to the reader, define his/her relationship to the piece being reviewed, express his/her considered opinion by giving appropriate evidence for it, and do it all with style—i.e. the reviews should be well-written,*

> *although the quality of the writing should only serve the discussion of the work being reviewed, rather than the display of the writer him/herself.*[10]

According to the British theatre critic Irving Wardle, the moral inflection in aesthetic judgment characteristic of British theatre criticism was an inheritance from seventeenth century Puritan England and the excesses of the Restoration era that followed, coupled with an inherent conservatism.[11] Radosavljević notes the 'remarkable compliance of British theatre critics in relationship to the establishment'—their reluctance, for example, with very few exceptions, to agitate in the 1950s and 1960s against the censorship laws. A not unrelated observation is that British theatre critics were, until as late as the 1990s, entirely male.

Australian theatre criticism, sedulously shaping itself as a colonial reflection of the motherland, inherited almost all of the characteristics and assumptions of British criticism. But there were crucial differences. Cultural criticism has never had the same prestige in Australia as it did in Britain or the US. Consequently, some bastions were easier to breach. Katharine Brisbane, notably a woman and arguably the most important Australian theatre critic of the late twentieth century, became national theatre critic for *The Australian* newspaper in 1967. Later, in the brief but extraordinary efflorescence of creativity that was theatre blogging culture in the early 2000s, it took less than four years for blog reviews to become accepted as mainstream. In

Britain, despite *The Guardian's* regular publication of theatre bloggers, this process took much longer, and was far more vexed. In the United States, it barely happened at all.

While it lasted, this historical moment opened possibilities in Australian performance criticism that simply hadn't existed before. I will now leap forward to the twenty-first century to examine it in detail.

2. Digital disruption

I remember when I first saw a computer in a newspaper office. It was the early 1980s, and I was a cadet reporter on the now defunct afternoon newspaper, the *Melbourne Herald*. What I saw was a huge, grey machine with a tiny screen, showing a Matrix-style green text on a black background.

None of us had any idea of the change that this machine would usher in. At first it didn't affect journalists. The first professions to go were printing jobs: those of the workers who lived on the floor above the editorial department in Flinders Street. They were compositors, their fingers shaped like spatulas from years of pressing the heavy keys of the hot-metal machines. Many of them had inherited their job from their fathers, and had expected to continue until the end of their working lives. But by 1987 their profession had vanished entirely, along with those of their colleagues: linotype operators, machine-room personnel, publishing-room employees, clerical staff and copytakers.

Rupert Murdoch was, as he so often is, at the forefront of this disruption. Print unions in Britain went on strike to preserve the jobs of more than 5,000 workers who were summarily sacked when Murdoch stealth-moved his operations to a plant in Wapping. This culminated in the year-long Wapping strike, one of the most bitter and violent industrial disputes of the past fifty years. During the strike opposing journalists were bussed in, crossing barbed-wire picket lines to bring out Murdoch's newspapers with the new technology. As a union official, Barry Fitzpatrick told *The Guardian* in 2006, following as it did on the hard-fought and doomed miners' strike, Wapping broke the back of union power in Britain:

> *Week in, week out, I attended the demonstrations and as the weeks turned to months, I watched the lives of people I'd known and worked with for years unravel. There were suicides, marriage break-ups; people lost their homes. Twenty years may have passed but those sacked overnight—secretaries, researchers and cashiers as well as printers—still bear the scars of Wapping today.*
>
> *The strike ended after a long bloody year, but the consequences of Murdoch's victory are still felt by the industry today. Other employers rushed to exploit the opportunities he'd opened up. When it comes to cutting costs and creaming off bigger profits, newspaper bosses have slavishly followed Murdoch's example.*[12]

This dispute is often seen as the turning point, when the 'bean counters' took power in the world of journalism. It's probably not much compensation to those workers who lost the struggle then, but now the journalists who broke the picket lines, and were instrumental in defeating the strike, are in the same position as the compositors in the 1980s. The past few years have been convulsive in Australian newspapers, with succeeding waves of job-shedding from all major titles. Partly this has been a result of advertising revenue moving online, and non-publishing platforms of distribution such as Google and Facebook gaining the lion's share of the advertising dollar. But a lot of advertising revenue—notably that from real estate—remained with the print mastheads (for example, the lucrative Domain group, founded by Fairfax Media and now owned by Channel Nine).

The real difference is that the advertising 'rivers of gold' that once financed journalism now flow to the shareholders, and 'content'—once known as 'journalism'— is merely the shell that seduces the eyeballs of readers for advertisers. Digital journalism is driven by increasingly sophisticated consumer analysis that can not only track how many people read an article, but for how long they read it. This means that that the 'public good' aspect of journalism has come into direct conflict with commercial imperatives. The fact that they ran side-by-side for so many years was, it turns out, merely a happy historical accident.

Arts journalism, and particularly arts criticism, has been one of the major casualties of these seismic shifts in the media industries. Their specialist, niche readerships meant that they were among the first to reduce or disappear under the reign of the bean counters and the laser-accurate reader stats of the data revolution. In

Australia, only newspapers that value the aura of prestige that comes with the arts—such as News Ltd's *The Australian*, or Schwartz Media's *Saturday Paper*—keep a strong arts section. Elsewhere, longform arts journalism has all but vanished from the mainstream press.

In the early 2000s, however, something fascinating happened. For a few years, between 2004 and 2012, there was a brief, anarchic window before the internet was fully corporatised. In this fortuitous bubble of time, online blogs, run mainly by individuals, could compete for audiences on something like a level playing field with the major print dailies. And this saw a golden period of theatre blogging and the rise of the amateur critic.

In Australia, and especially in Melbourne, there was a deeply invested, argumentative and lively community of theatre critic bloggers, many of them young. My own blog Theatre Notes, launched in 2004, was the first in Australia, and one of the first in the world. I wrote about the experience of running it for the literary magazine *Kill Your Darlings* in 2013, shortly after my blog closed. It is worth quoting at length because it goes to the heart of the change in both the status of the critic and the form of performance criticism—a change that Theatre Notes both reflected and facilitated.

Theatre Notes was an attempt to change the conversation. Miraculously, it did.

> *Since I closed the blog, there's been a lot of discussion on the place of criticism, especially for an ephemeral art form like performance, and how*

it can be financially sustained in the new, bleak media landscape. That's an important debate, especially for the younger generation of critics now emerging online; but it has nothing to do with why I started the blog, or why I decided to close it. Theatre Notes wasn't funded and was never dependent on institutional support; that was a very conscious decision on my part. What I valued above all in that writerly space was my autonomy, and I was very willing to pay for my freedom.

As a former journalist, I couldn't but be aware that the blog was a small part of a massive revolution: the rise of digital culture and the breaking of print's monopoly on the world of public ideas. It was a blog that took, if anything, a rather old-fashioned view of criticism, and exploited the new freedoms of the internet in order to explore it. It began on an impulse: I was at home, manacled to the desk writing a novel, and I was broke and bored with myself. And the thought lit up in my head: why not start a blog for theatre reviews? So I did […] In 2004, when I began Theatre Notes, I had little idea what had happened in Australian theatre in the twelve years since I'd given up criticism. There weren't many ways of finding out, either (which highlights the archival importance of performance criticism): aside from mostly unilluminating print reviews, the only really useful source was RealTime, *a pioneering print and internet journal that has covered innovative performance for 14 years.[…]*

I had no expectations; I didn't know whether anyone would read my blog, or even be interested.

As it turned out, over the next eight years people showed they were. Much of that came down to pure chance: I was the right person in the right place at the right time. The first reason was the poverty of theatre coverage. As a battle-scarred veteran of Melbourne theatre once commented to me, back in his day the most you could expect as a response to your work was a few indifferent paragraphs in The Age *and, at best, a small but thoughtful notice in* The Melbourne Times. *Then it fell into a memory hole and was never heard of again. The high concentration of media ownership in Australia—the highest in the western world—meant that there were very few outlets for critical response. There was a gap that was screaming to be filled, a hunger for thoughtful, longform, immediate response that reached beyond the standard consumer review. I was very aware of that lack, and determined Theatre Notes would address it.*

The other reason is more interesting. In the end, a critic is only as good as the work she writes about; and I was fortunate enough to find the work to review. Although I didn't know it, as I was having my private lightbulb moment in my study Melbourne theatre was about to change out of recognition. In 2004 the Playbox Theatre, the second largest subsidised theatre in Melbourne,

> *was artistically moribund, playing to houses of around 30 per cent capacity. In one of the most significant appointments for Australian theatre in the past decade, the board called in Michael Kantor, a freelance director-about-town, and Stephen Armstrong, a producer with a track record ranging from independent theatre to a tenure at the Sydney Theatre Company, to be respectively artistic director and executive producer. Digging into energies always present but long marginalised, they proceeded to redefine the mainstream Australian stage.*[13]

Looking back now, it's impossible to overestimate the importance of this change. Work that had been for two decades the province of the 'fringe', work in found spaces or tiny theatres, with perhaps a distant prospect of a moment in the spotlight before it vanished, was invited onto the main stage. Artists whose skills had been dismissed by an overwhelmingly conservative culture were suddenly centre stage, with the critical resources they needed to realise their potential. This resonated far beyond the newly named Malthouse Theatre itself: young independent companies had something to aim for or react against; and audiences who had thought the theatre on offer on the main stages as dusty as a Remington typewriter woke up.

When the Malthouse launched its first show in 2005—a double bill of Patrick White's *The Ham Funeral* and an adaptation by Tom Wright of Daniel Defoe's

Journal of a Plague Year—I wrote with excitement and relief:

> *It is a breath of fresh air to see mainstream theatre with ambition and intellectual clout, and that takes itself seriously as an art. I have no doubt this shift in artistic direction will generate a lot of controversy; Helen Thomson's bitterly hostile reviews in* The Age *this week are probably symptomatic. I also have no doubt that this new phase at Malthouse is the best thing that's happened there in the past decade; and as a theatre goer, I am hoping that this is only the beginning of a more generous imagining of the Australian stage.*[14]

This hopefulness turned out to be no chimera. Between 2004 and 2010 independent theatre flowered into a remarkable renaissance. Of course, this kind of shift never happens without resistance. In Australia, the reluctance to embrace new work can be particularly obdurate. The new might fight its way to the front, but how to stay there is another question. A telling example is director Jim Sharman's radical appointment to the State Theatre Company of South Australia, which he renamed the Lighthouse Theatre. He assembled an extraordinary ensemble cast that included Geoffrey Rush, Robert Menzies and Kerry Walker and premiered plays from Patrick White, Louis Nowra and Stephen Sewell, in seasons that are now the stuff of legend. The Lighthouse lasted only from 1982–83. And although its legacy still resonates through the culture (for one thing, it kick-started the distinguished career of Neil Armfield, who was later appointed director of Sydney's Belvoir St Theatre and today is co-artistic director of the Adelaide Festival) it's impossible not to look back and to see it as an opportunity lost, a possibility that briefly flared and died.

At the time, I saw this repressive mechanism at work in the consistent press attacks on the Malthouse's programming policies (and on other institutions that were bringing welcome vitality to the culture, such as Kristy Edmunds's Melbourne International Arts Festivals 2005–08, or some of the more outrageous young companies that were emerging in Melbourne). There was, as I saw at the time, no reason why the same fate as attended the Lighthouse might not happen to the Malthouse. But this time a radical reimagining didn't fail its promise, and the internet, by providing a public space for alternative views, was an important part of that. The monopoly of received opinion was over.

As a young theatre critic I had often been baffled by the apathy or outright hostility that usually greeted what for me was the most exciting work. I didn't believe it was a conscious conspiracy, but I had already noted how indifferent criticism could erase accomplishment, rebuke the new for challenging received wisdom, and assert authority in order to forbid discussion. Theatre Notes and the other blogs that sprang up in the following years began a conversation that invited difference, that spurred interest, that argued fiercely and (at its best) without rancour about ideas, aesthetics and politics. And gradually, instead of being the only public truth available, the corporate authority that trumps all others, the conservative mainstream pundit became only one voice among many.

From the beginning Theatre Notes was militantly against the silencing of art and debate, and the insistence on 'business as usual' which had characterised, with a number of notable exceptions, the generality of Australian arts criticism and sometimes arts institutions themselves. There have always been critics who saw their task to be a critical advocate or purveyor of ideas—Katharine Brisbane, co-founder of Currency Press and one of the most passionate campaigners for new Australian theatre through the 1970s, is a case in point. But they were rare.

More common were the kinds of critics who believed themselves to be the final word on a show, holding themselves above the audience and pronouncing judgment from on high. This was held to be unchallengeable: the critic was the ultimate patriarchal authority, and the childlike artist was presumed to be unqualified to make critical judgments of their own. For such critics, the only thing that counts is the imprimatur of approval or rejection. Yet that imprimatur remains the most boring aspect of reviews. The distinguished American critic and theatre practitioner Robert Brustein—one of the major influences behind Theatre Notes—described this well during a roundtable on criticism and its purpose as:

> *[trying] to find out what these artists, if they were artists, were trying to do, and then to see whether they did that successfully. But at least to try and find out what the intention was before I rejected it.*[15]

This was exactly what I attempted to practise: a criticism which employed my experience as a writer and sometime practitioner in the theatre, in order to form a response that was 'helpful and useful'. It carried an important rider: 'helpful and useful' doesn't mean being 'kind' or 'supportive'. Often it meant the reverse. Unwarranted praise has no place in rigorous criticism and is of no use to anyone, artist or audience.

I was a very particular kind of theatre critic. I saw (and see) myself as an advocate and, in some ways, a custodian with a shared responsibility for the wider culture. Moreover, I was the kind of critic that simply couldn't exist in Australian newspapers, then or now, forging a kind of criticism that also couldn't exist. Alongside younger commentators who entered the fray with their own blogs—Jana Perkovic, Jane Howard, Andrew Furhmann, Matthew Clayfield and others—and bloggers in Britain and the US such as Andrew Haydon, George Hunka, Isaac Butler, Megan Vaughan, Chris Goode and Matt Trueman, Theatre Notes became part of an online conversation that straddled conventional divisions between professional and amateur; critic, artist and audience; academic and popular; local and global.

Megan Vaughan described the nature of arts criticism in the digital age in a letter to Natasha Tripney in 2015:

> *It does kinda feel like those of us working on the internet have a responsibility to exercise all the freedoms it gives us to play with words and structure and forms, because criticism should be a LANDSCAPE. Digital criticism, for me, is the freedom to be different, but implicit in that is an obligation to be different, for the sake of a healthy culture of discourse, now and in the future.*[16]

The culture of 'an obligation to be different' took particular purchase in Australia. A major reason was the concentration of media ownership that has shaped public discussion in this country, especially after the Murdoch forces began their takeover of the print media in the 1980s. This concentration is today among the highest in the developed world.

As Murdoch's News Ltd consolidated its hold on the newspaper industry through the 1990s, cities which once had two or three daily newspapers found themselves, through a process of ongoing economic rationalisation, served by only one. News Ltd and Fairfax gradually bought almost every independent newspaper outlet, enabling these corporate entities to dominate the discourse throughout Australia's suburbs and regions.

This concentration of media ownership has meant a continually narrowing bottleneck, not only of information, but of opinion and criticism. This has had a massive impact on the arts in Australia, which have, unlike the European nations, a comparatively slender and dependent tradition of arts commentary. Even before Murdoch, the public fortunes of a theatre company were at the mercy of a tiny number of print critics. This critic, whatever their qualifications, carried all the authority of the institution they worked for, and their views were seldom publicly questioned.

In the early 2000s, the internet made possible two important developments. One was the return of the genuinely independent critic. Chicago film critic Roger Ebert, for example, claimed that the digital age ushered in a 'golden age' of film criticism.[17] Simply because they could, a lot of intelligent people went online and started writing about the stuff they saw. They had no need for an institution to make their work visible to the public. They could write whatever they liked, and get it out to an audience, and it cost them no more than an internet connection.

Freed from the word limitations of print media, they could consider things in detail. Freed from the newspaper style guide and vocabulary, our critic could bring as much complexity to the contemplation of art as they liked. I remember Andrew Furhmann's early reviews, which were conducted entirely in Symposia-like dialogues. One in particular was just a series of diagrams. There were long and impassioned comment threads between enthusiasts about particular productions, which in turn teased out intellectual arguments over thousands of words. Perkovic's blog Guerilla Semiotics, for example, published a discussion of Simon Stone's production of *The Wild Duck* that went for almost 10,000 words beneath her original review.[18] There were theatre reviews which consisted entirely of gifs. Everything suddenly became possible.

There was a heady freedom to all this. These critics were able to bring to the immediate work of review a richer vocabulary of thought and a broader notion of form than was ever possible in newspapers. The sudden prominence of this sort of critic, who simply wrote about art because they wanted to, broke the monopoly of the mass media with astonishing swiftness. And for a while, the diversity of response matched the diversity of the work that was made.

The second important thing was that those who never had a public voice, the audience themselves, could now add their two cents to the polyphony. It is worth recalling Enzensberger's aphorism here about word of mouth, 'which is both free and beyond price'. Their interventions might range from an idle tweet to a deeply engaged blog post. The distinction between the professional critic and the amateur commentator became blurred. The reader/audience member was the most common sort of arts blogger and, as the publishing industry discovered, they had a lot of power. Opinions once confined to the private domain were now out in public for others to read.

Among other things, the growth of theatre blogs threw into sharp relief the double standard that underlay a great deal of cultural production, and which has existed for centuries as both an amateur and a professional pursuit. The word 'amateur' usually carries a derogatory tone, meaning unskilled, ignorant or second-rate. And it's a word with economic baggage: an 'amateur' is unpaid, whereas the 'professional' is paid. A pay cheque is the badge and boon of professionalism, with money the currency of intellectual status. If you were unpaid, so conventional wisdom went, you didn't know what you were talking about.

This distinction was used often by journalists and critics to attack bloggers—the cliché was that a blogger was an ignorant, asocial nerd banging away on his computer in his (again, the default was male) basement. The print journalist or critic had trained, professional skills; the blogger parasitically (and anonymously) exploited the paid work of the professional and used it to puff up his amateur ego, along the way undermining the whole profession. Andrew Marr, former political editor of the BBC, wasn't untypical when he said in 2010:

> *A lot of bloggers seem to be socially inadequate, pimpled, single, slightly seedy, bald, cauliflower-nosed young men sitting in their mother's basements and ranting. They are very angry people. OK—the country is full of very angry people. Many of us are angry people at times. Some of us are angry and drunk. But the so-called citizen journalism is the spewings and rantings of very drunk people late at night. It is fantastic at times but it is not going to replace journalism.*[19]

This amateur/professional division is a distinction that

breaks down as soon as you get anywhere near artists. Auden once commented that poets had no idea of the value of money, because they could spend a year writing a poem that earns them ten dollars and an afternoon writing an essay that earns them five hundred. Brecht wanted professional status badly: he wrote his second play, *Drums in the Night*, to earn a buck while he was a struggling medical student, and is said to have erupted into fury when an older playwright told him he had written a stunning work of art. That wasn't what he had intended at all. The history of art is replete with (romanticised) stories of artists dying of poverty in garrets. Rembrandt, for example, lived his later years in desperate poverty, but painted his greatest work at that time. He was clearly no less skilled when he was unpaid than when he was paid.

Art and a steady income are not mutually exclusive, and poverty is not a badge of integrity, any more than an income is a mark of 'selling out'. Artists, as a matter of principle, ought to be paid for their work, but the reality in our world is that very often they are not. Every artist wants to earn a living, and maybe the biggest challenge in an artist's life is economic survival. Every working artist knows that, whether they like it or not, the biggest subsidy for the arts comes from the unpaid labour of artists themselves. In the strict economic division of professional versus amateur, most artists qualify as amateur.

However, there is another dimension to the word 'amateur'. Amateur derives from the Latin verb *amare*, to love. It also signifies a commitment to a vocation that is pursued for its own sake, rather than for the sake of money. In the nineteenth century, the amateur sportsman was a fiercely guarded ideal, especially among the privileged classes, and for much of the twentieth century only amateurs—those who did not derive income from sport—were permitted to compete in the Olympics.

This amateur status is, out of necessity, still alive and well in the arts. Australian culture would, in fact as well as in spirit, collapse without the unpaid work of the many. We certainly wouldn't have a theatre culture in Australia without it. Early companies like the New Theatre in Sydney, Melbourne and Brisbane, formed in the 1930s, or the 'alternative' theatre revolution of the 1970s, were fuelled by precisely this kind of unpaid but highly committed work. Only the most privileged can make a full-time living from making art.

This ambiguous status has been generally recognised by such things as labelling co-op independent theatres 'semi-professional' or 'independent', but it remains an uncomfortable division. It's too easily hijacked into an *a priori* judgment on the kind of work it signifies as being less important or achieved less than that of 'professional' companies. And again, a swift gallop through the history of art—even a quick look at the past few decades of Australian theatre—demonstrates that artistic significance, merit and skill don't correlate with whether the artist had been paid for their work.

Amateur and professional are not, clearly, neutral descriptors. They both come with a lot of baggage.

They are most commonly used as markers of status: a professional writer has a higher status, for example, than an amateur. Much of the usage of these terms, in other words, has been about shoring up and reinforcing privilege. This partly explains why the internet, with its sudden democratisation of opinion, gave rise to such anxiety, especially in those professions already feeling under attack in the massive cultural shifts of the previous decades.

Typically, media coverage about the death of critical authority generally pointed the finger of blame in one of two places: increasingly alienating erudition on the one hand, and/or the noisy democracy of the internet on the other. Writing in *The Guardian* in 2007, Rónán McDonald, summed up this argument:

> *The critic has a vital role to play in culture and one that is under threat. When Samuel Beckett's play* Waiting for Godot *was first produced on the London stage in 1955, it was greeted with derision [...] But when favourable reviews appeared in the Sunday papers by the leading theatre critics Kenneth Tynan and Harold Hobson, the play was taken seriously.* Waiting for Godot *is now regarded as the most important play of the twentieth century. Controversial artists have often been brought to a resistant public by prominent critics [...] But are there now critics of sufficient authority to perform this role?*
>
> *Is this because we are all critics now? There has*

> *been a tremendous democratisation in response to the arts [...] the idea that one opinion is as good as another has accelerated in recent years [...] Alongside the popular expansion of criticism, the academic study of the arts has become much more specialised and esoteric [...] academics are content to speak to each other in technical language, published in small-circulation journals. The popular widening of criticism and its academic contraction might seem opposites but are in fact symptoms of the same assumption: that artistic value is simply a question of personal taste. The critic-as-instructor, as objective judge and expert, has yielded to the critic who shares personal reactions and subjective enthusiasms.*[20]

This assumes several things about the critic, not least 'his' authority (it's not a coincidence that many online critics are women and, increasingly, people of colour). McDonald defends 'the critic-as-instructor, as objective judge and expert', the taste-maker who decides what will and will not enter the canon of great works. He has a valid point—the most important work a critic can do is to create a context in which new or challenging work can be appreciated. What he ignores, in claiming full credit for the perception of critics in advocating for art that doesn't immediately catch the public taste, is the power of the art itself.

In this picture is the presumption that the only person in the audience with an acute and superior sensitivity to art *is* the critic. The critic descends to sit among the hoi polloi and dispense his wisdom to the masses, who otherwise would just boo and catcall.

This is too narrow a view. An artist's work might be *recognised* by a critic, and that has often been an important step for their work in reaching a wider public. But equally, if they are to have a legacy, it's important that others—an audience, no matter how small—are fired by the same enthusiasm: in other words, that the work means something to those who experience it. If a work of art doesn't express something that someone else feels deeply, then no amount of critical pumping will preserve it in the cultural memory. The only reason why we can read Sappho's poems in the twenty-first century is because an anonymous monk loved them enough to rescue them from the destruction of the Library of Constantinople in the great fire of 473 CE. Equally, phalanxes of critics writing vitriolic negative reviews have done nothing to stop Cameron Mackintosh making millions from his musicals.

There are all sorts of works of art, and infinite means of making and experiencing them. Criticism and response have always been—and to my mind remain, even in this volatile age of information deluge—a means of processing, sorting and understanding, of providing the grounds for discrimination. As crucially as it is an individual activity, it is a collective process. Criticism as a whole is best recognised as a polyphony, rather than a monologue. If there is diversity in making and experiencing art, then the health of cultural response can be measured by the availability of a social diversity of response.

This is not the same as claiming that 'one opinion is as good as another'. I don't think that about art, and I don't think it about arts criticism. But it does mean that the process of assigning value is much more complex than deferral to the authority of a single critical voice.

3. The Age of SEO

I'm not utopian about digital technology. Anyone wanting to make a case for the decadence of late capitalist culture need only go online. There, you can find every sort of proof of human greed, ignorance, foolishness, cruelty and criminality. The internet made possible phenomena such as WikiLeaks, which seek to destroy the conspiracy of governance by a militant openness. Equally, it allows secret police all over the world to locate and arrest dissenters and it enabled both the rise and the fall of Julian Assange. It is an extremely powerful tool, which can be employed in many ways.

As far as arts culture was concerned, the first effect of the digital revolution was the destablisation of hierarchies of taste. Instead of the critic being at the top of the heap, the internet created an intensely complex system of interconnected networks of opinion. Those wanting to adhere to the old, stable authorities often found themselves lost and bewildered. The discourse became fluid and rapid, and energies moved according to different and sometimes counter-intuitive rules. The only imperative—and this still holds—is participation.

Artistic institutions became aware of those who encountered their work in ways they had never done before and critics could be challenged and argued with.

What was new was not the existence of this opinion, but its public airing. People have always had opinions. For as long as there have been theatres, audience members have been star struck, or have muttered darkly as they left the foyer. It might not be 'reviewing' *per se*, but it is, and always has been, part of the chattiness around art. And, after all, what's so bad about listening to what audiences have to say? The arts company prepared to listen and genuinely participate could learn a lot about the people seeing their work, and more, could build up an invaluable fount of goodwill, an active relationship, with their audiences.

What the internet meant during the blogging era was that more people were talking about art. They were talking about it because it moved them—it angered them, or pleased or excited them. They connected in small, volatile communities, some lasting a microsecond, others enduring for years. They were not waiting—if they ever did—for some authority to tell them what they thought. Some spoke from areas of deep expertise; others from lack of experience; but that was just the beginning of a conversation. As an arts manager once said to me, 'Anything is better than the white death of silence'. The discussion online was the sound of vitality.

But all good things—including individual blogs—come to an end. It was inevitable that the freedom the internet made possible would be constrained. Blogs, for the most part, have been absorbed into larger online organisations, and have lost almost all their distinctive anarchy.

The landscape has changed again. We are now in a world dominated by social media companies such as Facebook and Twitter, and an online topography dominated by the giants of the data age, Google, Facebook and Amazon. It's the age of the online search engine and Search Engine Optimisation (SEO), a highly lucrative industry in which people spend millions making themselves visible on Google.

So what went wrong?

It isn't possible anymore, as it was in 2004, to launch a tiny niche web page and accidentally build a wide international audience. There are a number of reasons for this, but the major one is probably financial. For most people, it's too hard to sustain the unpaid work an online blog requires. In my case, I could write for Theatre Notes because I was making a good wage from my novels. I was a 'mid list' novelist, who made a living from my books. Over the past decade, as the digital disruption convulsed the publishing industry, the mid-list novelist has all but disappeared. I can't afford to blog for free anymore.

In 2014, two years after I closed Theatre Notes, I wrote an overview of theatre criticism for Australian Plays, the online portal for play scripts that now, in a symptom of the austerity that is currently strangling smaller arts organisations, is facing closure after it was refused four-year funding by the Australia Council. It was the moment to consider the status of theatre criticism, whether it had genuinely changed, or merely varied:

> *The one thing you can say with certainty about the business of theatre criticism over the past decade is that it's been volatile. In Australia, the initial excitement of the digital revolution is now well over. Over the past couple of years the rise of substantial online arts portals, from ABC Arts Online, to The Guardian, to Crikey's Daily Review, to Time Out, to ArtsHub, means there is suddenly a plethora of outlets for arts reviewing, which to some degree makes up for diminishing coverage in mainstream mastheads.*
>
> *But has anything really changed? I'm not sure. In all the panic about shrinking opportunities, how much have we reimagined what criticism is, and what it could be?*[21]

I noted a number of problems: a lack of diverse voices, especially those of non-Anglo Australia; the continual question of how to financially sustain critical practice; and the cutting back of coverage in the mainstream press, which especially affects dance and independent theatre. In particular, I noted that the struggle to find a place for sustained and in-depth critical engagement remains as difficult as ever:

> *Recently debate has atomised further, into social media—it often occurs through the ephemeralities*

> *of Facebook and Twitter, rather than the passionate online debates that characterised Melbourne theatre criticism at its best. It means the discussion that does exist is harder to track and access for anyone not immediately aware of it. Meanwhile, as the anarchic culture of blogs is folded into corporate sites, attracting writers who are grateful to be paid, however little, for their work, the consumer guide review remains unchallenged. We're scoring shows out of five, as if we're marking maths tests in primary school. We're writing brief reviews that can't begin to consider the ideas offered in the work we're seeing. The possibilities, not for reviewing itself, but for real critical engagement, seem as limited as they ever were.*

Five years on, these problems have only grown. As always, the niche activity of live performance criticism reflects much larger cultural shifts. A major factor is the ongoing convulsions in the media, as journalists' jobs continually disappear. In the past five years, we've been watching the end game of the printer strikes in the last century.

Fairfax journalists have been fighting and losing for years. They went on strike in 2014 to protest the loss of 80 jobs. They went on strike again in 2016, to protest 120 redundancies, and again in 2017, when a further 125 jobs were lost. (Since 2012, in fact, Fairfax has shed more than 2000 jobs.) Domain, the profitable real estate arm of Fairfax, was listed as a separate company on the Australian Stock Exchange in November 2017, effectively removing the richest advertising revenue from journalism, although Fairfax retained a 60 per cent stake. Finally, in July last year, Channel Nine revealed a $2.2 billion friendly takeover of Fairfax (with projected cost savings of $50 million).

In each of these waves, arts journalism jobs were, as they usually are, among the first to go. In 2017, the #FairGoFairfax campaign, pushed by arts celebrities during a week-long strike, highlighted the loss of arts jobs. Fairfax planned to sack all dedicated arts, film and books writers at *The Age* and *The Sydney Morning Herald*, make two deputy arts editor roles defunct, and cut contributor rates by about half.[22] It's a similar story at News Corp Australia, with waves[23] of redundancies[24] over the past few years.

Along with jobs, the space dedicated to arts reporting and discussion has been continually shrinking since the 1990s. When I was Melbourne theatre critic for *The Bulletin* in the early nineties, an average review was 800 words. By 2000 in the same publication, it was 500. In 2009, when I was reviewing for *The Australian*, reviews were 400 words. Now it's not uncommon to see reviews in Fairfax publications, once a bastion of mainstream arts coverage, of under 200 words.

Meanwhile, other arts outlets were facing difficulties and closing. *RealTime*—a journal of experimental art critique founded by Keith Gallasch and Virginia Baxter that was generously funded by the Australia Council—closed after 24 years in 2018. At the same time, the classical music and performance magazine *Limelight*—sold by the ABC's Classic FM to entrepreneur Andrew Batt-Rawden's Arts Initiative Pty Ltd in 2014—ran into financial difficulties and faced closure. It was rescued by two Sydney businessmen, Robert Veel and Bruce Watson.

There have been some moves to combat this in the public realm, but the pressures on our public broadcaster since the election of a Coalition federal government in 2013 put paid to that. In 2012, the ABC's Head of Arts, Katrina Sedgwick, decided that the broadcaster should begin to pick up the slack on the vanishing space for critique, and appointed a number of arts critics, including myself, to write for ABC Arts Online.

Sedgwick resigned in 2015, after the first wave of LNP cuts, which saw my job, among others, disappear. But now even the records are gone. In 2017, ABC Arts Online's entire archive—including reviews, commissioned films and features, amounting to hundreds of thousands of dollars' worth of work—simply vanished offline, demonstrating the vulnerability of digital memory. There was a muted outcry, which saw their brief return and repeat disappearance. To date there is no sign that any of that work will return from the memory hole.

Back in 2004, I thought of on-line criticism as an alternative to mainstream theatre critique, a complementary role that supplemented the shorter, product-oriented reviews that existed in the larger media. That idea now seems almost quaint. The collapse of arts critique in the mainstream media means that online critique is often the only alternative there is, if it exists at all. It is common for many shows—especially contemporary dance, which typically has short seasons—to get no critical notice, and the notion of a sustained, engaged, thoughtful critical culture seems as far away as it ever did. A successful commercial site such as ArtsHub relies on a mixture of membership, sponsored content, advertising and, in particular, job advertisements, and its coverage is driven by the same SEO-driven metrics that inform commercial media organisations. This means that the focus is increasingly on topical stories or listicles with an ideal length of around 400 words. It serves a useful function as an industry news hub, but its emphasis is not on critique. Tellingly, at ArtsHub all the critics, aside from journalists on staff who are nevertheless not renumerated for the extra time it takes to review, are unpaid.

Over 2017 and 2018, quite independently, three new online sites focusing on arts criticism sprang up in three different cities as a response to the ongoing crisis: *Witness Performance* in Melbourne, founded by myself and the theatre historian, playwright and director Robert Reid; *Audrey Journal* in Sydney, founded by husband and wife team Elissa and Jason Blake, formerly arts journalists and critics for *The Sydney Morning Herald*; and *Seesaw* magazine in Perth, founded by arts writers Nina Levy and Varnya Bromilow, now co-edited by Levy and Rosalind Appleby.

Each journal has a different take on the model of arts critique and different models of financing itself. Running a website is a lot of work, requiring organisational, financial and promotional skills, and, as independent sites, *Audrey*, *Seesaw* and *Witness* are run by two or three people who wear most of those hats. All of them are currently unpaid, and all of them are tired.

Each website has been successful in their coverage and in finding readerships (*Witness's* readership on single pages is on par with much larger and better resourced websites) and this to some extent has compensated for the loss of coverage in the mainstream media. But as opposed to fifteen years ago, websites such as *Audrey* are trying to *replace* the missing print arts coverage, rather than complement it.

Audrey is a magazine-style publication with features and reviews, and a large number of contributors. It was launched with philanthropic seed funding that lasted six months, Sydney theatre companies contributing in a tiered membership model, with small contributions tied to interviews with major creatives. They successfully applied for a City of Sydney grant that pays for two or three reviews a week, with funding that runs to the middle of next year.

Witness focuses on longform reviews and features. It works on a subscriber model, with some sponsorship, but the bulk of its funding so far has come from three small project grants—two from Creative Victoria, and a 2018 grant from the Australia Council. The grant money ran out in June 2019, which means, as with *Audrey*, the editors are working for no pay, although contributors and expenses are still covered by other sources.

Seesaw, which is a response to the paucity of any kind of arts critique in Perth, reviews across art forms and is almost entirely a voluntary enterprise. They have succeeded in raising small amounts of funding, and are awaiting the outcome of an application for state funding that would mean they could pay themselves and contributors over the January/February festival season. 'It's frustrating to hear people tell us how important it is that we keep going, while not realising that we have no resources,' says Levy. 'And I'm finding it hard to stay on top of what needs to be done for the website, because I need to take freelance work in order to make ends meet.'[25]

Importantly, each website also mentors new critics—an aspect crucial to the future of criticism. *Witness* ran the New Review program last year that mentored four critics from Footscray Arts Centre's West Writers, and has appointed a First Nations Emerging Critic for the past two years. In less formal ways, we also have brought new voices into the discourse, notably First Nations and disabled writers, including the first theatre reviews by a Blind writer that, to my knowledge, have been published anywhere.

We've led discussion on many issues, such as the issue of sexual harassment in Australian theatre (*Witness* was the first publication to raise the issue in 2017 and my essay on the Rush trial appears in the recent #MeToo anthology, published this year by Picador[26]). We have a proud record of publishing new perspectives from marginalised writers. It is a well-known fact throughout the Australian media that the major reason that Indigenous issues and writers aren't published is because Indigenous content doesn't 'get the numbers'. We have made an explicit decision not to follow these commercial imperatives.

Audrey also emphasises diversity in its critical coverage and has been mentoring new voices. 'We are developing a handful of new critics,' says Blake.

> *They are promising. But we can't find new voices who are keen or willing to see theatre four to five nights a week in the way the current batch of critics do. It just doesn't pay well enough and it won't lead to a career as a paid theatre critic.*[27]

Levy voices similar problems, in their case exacerbated by their inability to pay their critics, which makes it difficult to retain talented writers and impossible to demand punctuality.

What is clear from the adventures of the past two years is that finding financial support for critical work is a huge challenge. The mantra is 'sustainability', which means that funding is predicated on turning the business into a flourishing commercial enterprise. But as the adventures in news media show dramatically, arts reporting—and especially critique—*isn't* commercial. *Witness*, *Audrey* and *Seesaw* are all passion projects, driven by people responding to a genuine crisis in critical coverage. But none of us can continue to work indefinitely without pay.

At *Witness* we could, of course, change our modus operandi and accept advertising, which we decided not to do when we launched because of the many cases in which the threat of its withdrawal has been used to silence critical voices. We could obey the conventions of SEO and stop running longform articles and critiques in favour of shorter, more clickbaity pieces, and abandon historical essays altogether. But that would negate the very reasons we started the site in the first place. We launched in order to provide a place for longer, in-depth investigations, for critical discussion, for historical perspective. Our mission is to stimulate thinking about performance as an art rather than a product. If we can't do those things, what's the point of our existing at all?

The difficulty of finding support for critical work is linked to the general crisis in arts funding in Australia. Six years of LNP government without any kind of clear arts policy has made its attritional impact: as with every other aspect of Australian society, power and money in the arts have gravitated to a privileged elite at the expense of the marginalised and poor.

There was, most spectacularly, the 2015 raid of then Arts Minister Senator George Brandis, which took $104 million out of the Australia Council's discretionary budget for his National Programme for Excellence in the Arts. Although some of the money came back (eventually), $25 million disappeared altogether. By April next year, the number of small-to-medium organisations with multi-year federal funding is expected to be less than

100, compared to 178 in 2013: barely half of what was funded only six years ago.

In the context of ongoing cuts and further, more insidious funding cuts—the 'efficiency dividend' imposed on all cultural institutions—and the invisible strangulation that comes with the non-indexation of arts funding (which means that, in real terms, it diminishes every year)—the future for the small-to-medium arts sector, and particularly for independent artists, looks very bleak. It makes it hard to argue for some of that precious funding to go to those organisations that merely write about art, rather than make it.

4. Why does this matter? Cultural criticism and cultural memory

It matters to artists. All artists desire to please their audience, but for most—myself included—what matters a great deal more than praise or blame is that someone has perceived, with accuracy and insight, exactly what you did.

Theatre Notes taught me many things, but perhaps the most important lesson was that just as indifferent criticism can be disabling, good criticism can be enabling. It carves out cultural space, makes connections, suggests further possibilities and opens generosities of perception. As more voices joined the many conversations over that decade, it became clear how critical dialogue could build a community invested in the performing arts, how it could be a link between artists and their audiences. Most importantly, perhaps, in this age of polarising communities, it demonstrated how differences of opinion could illuminate each other as part of a common sensibility and larger argument.

The brief interregnum of blogging opened up some exciting possibilities: a more generous view of public critical discourse that welcomed essential new voices and, with them, new ideas. The community of exchange that grew up around blogs—including artists, audience members and critics in the conversation—gave a glimpse of what criticism can do in a model driven not by commercial imperative but centred on the art itself. It demonstrated how critical dialogue can be the lifeblood of intellectual exchange, how it could be an energy that generates community and creates audiences for new work, how it could connect the present of the performing arts to its past, and throw open paths for its future.

These are the possibilities that sites such as *Audrey*, *Seesaw* and *Witness* seek to keep open, each in their own way. But for all of us, the costs of continuing what is an essential public service are mounting up. It seems to me one more aspect of the crisis in our cultural memory. In 2016, I wrote in *The Monthly* that the past three years have seen an unremitting ideological war on knowledge, inquiry and, significantly, cultural memory.[28] Three years later, it seems to me that this war on cultural memory has been all but lost by the increasingly exhausted people inside and outside institutions around Australia battling to keep it alive.

Cultural memory in our nation has always been limited. There are many reasons for this, but a major one is our lack of a robust tradition of public critical exchange. This particularly affects performance. As an ephemeral form, criticism constitutes its memory, and functions in many cases as its major historical record. The cultural amnesia that characterises our public knowledge of performance is exacerbated by the retreat of history as a discipline in our educational institutions: it's taught less and less. The less we remember, the more we are condemned to an ever-narrowing present. As Julian Meyrick pointed out in a Platform Paper in 2005:

> *Donald Horne's complaint that the industry's idea of cultural debate is a one-line telegram signed by twenty artists, points up the lack of articulated vision coming from theatre professionals on the ground today [...] At a recent public meeting on the future of Playbox [Theatre], I was not the only one struck by the lack of specific knowledge about the company we had come to discuss. And when, at the end, someone stood up— as someone always does— and said: 'Who needs the past anyway?'— as someone always does—a vision rose before my eyes of a wheel of fire on which Australian theatre was to be endlessly wracked, our historical forgetting a constituent part of our ongoing suffering.*[29]

In the current climate, the only public critique that flourishes is the atomised product-driven consumer review, which is more often a function of public relations than of serious intellectual enterprise. And that in turn reflects back on artmaking itself, influencing what is considered important and what isn't. And so on and so on, in an eternal circle.

What this impoverished and impoverishing critical discourse most commonly disadvantages is the new, the complex, the difficult, the exciting. Very often it ignores or misrepresents, even in well intentioned ways, the work of the marginalised: women, LGBTQI+ artists, CALD artists, especially from Australia's African and Asian diaspora, and Indigenous cultures. At the moment, it is busy characterising the decolonising impulse that is driving the most interesting art and thought happening in this country as self-interested 'identity politics', turning it into a weapon in the culture wars. But that's another Platform Paper.

Perhaps the most frustrating part of this argument is that everyone agrees that it's important to have a healthy, diverse critical culture. At *Audrey Journal*, *Seesaw* and *Witness*, we are all familiar with the voices that tell us how important it is that we continue, how essential the service we provide is to our local cultures. But if no-one pays for this service, it's simply not going to exist. Lip service is cheap.

It is clear to me now that we are witnessing the collapse of a model of criticism that has dominated in Anglo countries for centuries. As I outlined, it originally emerged in the 1700s as a colonial enterprise, shoring up ideas about nationhood and humanity that were conditioned by the adventuring of the British Empire. It was shaped by the intellectual discourse of that time, a discourse in which women and people of colour were assumed to be inherently inferior, and in which intellectual and aesthetic authority was vested exclusively in the European male.

These assumptions came under increasing stress in

the intellectual and political ferment of the twentieth century, a process that has accelerated since 2000 as the middle class steadily loses the economic and cultural status it gained under late capitalism.[30] In 2019, in every area of public discussion, we see those stresses metastasise into virulent symptoms of public anxiety and social and political conflict.

Public—as opposed to academic—performance criticism has long been seen as a subset of journalism, and its fate echoes that of journalism itself. As with the expensive, time-consuming work of investigative journalism or war reporting, the advent of the digital age has seen, with a few exceptions, its prestige dwindling to near invisibility.

The serial loss of arts pages in our major outlets presents problems for performing arts companies, beginning with the problem of letting their audiences know that a show is on. But beyond the dilemmas of public relations—which large companies solve by advertising and employing marketing staff—an entire body of arts journalism, let alone arts criticism, is increasingly absent from our national discussion. More seriously, because it's hard to see a future working as a performance critic, it's hard to attract and train the next generation of critics. Together with the absence of specialist publications that had previously existed, such as *Theatre Australia* and *RealTime*, this means that many live performances now get no critical response at all. The loss has especially affected the small independent companies where new ideas and new aesthetics are incubated.

A chance for a rethink?

This is a grim situation, in keeping with the larger shifts in arts funding that are placing pressure on even our largest cultural institutions. But the crisis could also give us the chance to rethink theatre criticism itself.

While there have been exceptions—Katharine Brisbane, Geraldine Pascall or Pamela Payne for example—most print critics in Australia have been, and remain, men. The emergence of critics who are Indigenous or from CALD backgrounds is even more recent, and largely a result of the democratisation of the digital age. If diversity in the arts is important—and it is, if the arts are to have purchase on the social issues and problems of our time—so is the diversity of our criticism.

This age of dolour is also a chance to bring performing arts criticism back into the purview of art. Because of its nature—its reporting of an event and its purpose as a consumer review—theatre reviewing has been dominated and shaped by journalistic conventions in ways that, for example, literary criticism hasn't. It's commonplace for novelists to review novels, whereas for a theatre critic to be a practitioner is usually considered to be a drawback: expertise is devalued as a conflict of interest. The expansive, art-centred advocacy and questioning commentary that practising artists such as Guillaume Apollinaire, Bernard Shaw, Frank O'Hara or, more recently, the English playwright and blogger Chris Goode, can bring to a critical discourse has been largely absent in Australian theatre criticism.

The biggest problem theatre criticism in Australia faces is simple economics. The unpalatable truth is that critical work—especially the longform in-depth reviewing that truly chronicles the evolution of the art—isn't and can't be commercial. Criticism is time-consuming, ill paid, difficult and often thankless, and critics have the career prospects of a chocolate kettle. Why should younger writers risk their futures on such a poor outlook?

Criticism, as the Mexican poet and critic Octavio Paz observed, is what makes a culture: without it, you just have a lot of art. For understandable reasons in the current climate it is the poor relation in any discussion about public funding. But criticism isn't an optional extra. Without it, our culture becomes a series of atomised acts that flicker into the privatised present and are then forgotten. If it is to survive in any but its most denatured forms, Australian cultural bodies now need to take this long-debated crisis in theatre criticism seriously, and to consider seriously how to support it.

Endnotes

All digital references accessed by the author valid at time of printing.

1 Joseph Roach, *Cities of the Dead: Circum-Atlantic Performance*, New York: Columbia University Press 1996 p.75.
2 Matthew White, *Newspapers, gossip and coffee-house culture*, https://www.bl.uk/restoration-18th-century-literature/articles/newspapers-gossip-and-coffee-house-culture
3 James Ley, *The Critic in the Modern World*, New York: Bloomsbury 2014 p.15.
4 James Ley, p.18.
5 John Brewer, *The Pleasures of the Imagination: English Culture in the Eighteenth Century*, London: Harper Collins 1997 p.16.
6 Hans Magnus Enzensberger, *Twilight of the Reviewers, Mediocrity and Delusion*, London: Verso 1992.
7 Duška Radosavljević (ed), *Theatre Criticism: Changing Landscapes*, London: Bloomsbury Methuen Drama 2016 p.6.
8 Radosavljević, p.6.
9 Foreword, Stella Gibbons, *Cold Comfort Farm*, Melbourne: Penguin Books Australia 2011.

10 Duška Radosavljević (ed), *Theatre Criticism: Changing Landscapes*, London: Bloomsbury Methuen Drama 2016 p.6.
11 Radosavljević, p.8.
12 'Wapping: legacy of Rupert's revolution', *Observer* 15 January 2006, https://www.theguardian.com/business/2006/jan/15/rupertmurdoch.pressandpublishing
13 Alison Croggon, 'Notes on Theatre Notes: The Importance of Being Seen', *Kill Your Darlings* No 13, April 2013.
14 Review: Alison Croggon, '*Ham Funeral* and *Journal of a Plague Year*', Theatre Notes, http://theatrenotes.blogspot.com.au/2005/04/ham-funeraljournal-of-plague-year.html
15 The Critic as Thinker: A discussion at the Philoctetes Center of New York City, http://www.tcg.org/publications/at/feb08/critics.cfm
16 Radosavljević, p.24.
17 Roger Ebert, 'The Golden Age of Movie Critics', 1 May 2010, https://www.rogerebert.com/rogers-journal/the-golden-age-of-movie-critics
18 Jana Perkovic, '*The Wild Duck*: The Slapified Ibsen' 10 March 2012, https://guerrillasemiotics.com/2012/03/the-wild-duck-the-slapified-ibsen-reviewessay/
19 Roy Greenslade, 'Marr on bloggers: inadequate, pimpled, single, seedy, abusive ranters', *The Guardian* 13 October 2010, https://www.theguardian.com/media/greenslade/2010/oct/11/andrewmarr-blogging
20 Rónán McDonald, 'A triumph of banality', *The*

Guardian 3 October 2007, https://www.theguardian.com/commentisfree/2007/oct/02/comment.art

21 Alison Croggon, 'The Critical Gap', Australian Plays, 29 April 2014, https://australianplays.org/the-critical-gap

22 Steph Harmon, 'Australian artists, writers and actors call on Fairfax Media not to cut arts coverage', 8 May2017, https://www.theguardian.com/media/2017/may/08/australian-artists-writers-and-actors-call-on-fairfax-media-not-to-cut-arts-coverage

23 Amanda Meade, 'News Corp Australia plans to axe journalists who lack digital skills', 4 June 2019, https://www.theguardian.com/media/2019/jun/04/news-corp-australia-plans-to-axe-journalists-without-digital-skills

24 Amanda Meade, 'News Corp Australia sacks most of its photographers and subeditors to cut costs', 1 April 2019, https://www.theguardian.com/media/2017/apr/11/news-corp-australia-sacks-most-of-its-photographers-and-subeditors-to-cut-costs

25 Personal communication with the author.

26 *#MeToo: Stories from the Australian Movement*, ed. Natalie Kon-yu, Christie Nieman, Maggie Scott and Miriam Sved, Sydney: Picador 2019.

27 Personal communication with the author.

28 Alison Croggon, 'Culture Crisis', *The Monthly* October 2016, https://www.themonthly.com.au/issue/2016/october/1475244000/alison-croggon/culture-crisis

29 Julian Meyrick, *Trapped by the Past: Why our*

Theatre is Facing Paralysis, Platform Paper 3, January 2005.

30 'Governments must act to help struggling middle class.' OECD 10 April 2019, https://www.oecd.org/newsroom/governments-must-act-to-help-struggling-middle-class.htm

COPYRIGHT INFORMATION

PLATFORM PAPERS
Quarterly essays from Currency House Inc.
Founding Editor: Dr John Golder
Editor: Katharine Brisbane
Currency House Inc. is a non-profit association and resource centre advocating the role of the performing arts in public life by research, debate and publication.

Postal address: PO Box 2270, Strawberry Hills, NSW 2012, Australia
Email: info@currencyhouse.org.au Tel: (02) 9319 4953
Website: www.currencyhouse.org.au Fax: (02) 9319 3649

ISBN 978 0 6484265 4 7
ISSN 1449-583X

Typeset in Garamond
Production by Currency Press Pty Ltd
Printed by Fineline Print + Copy Services, Revesby, NSW.

FORTHCOMING

PP No.62, February 2020

PERFORMING ARTS MARKETS
AND THEIR CONTRADICTIONS
Justin Macdonnell

The performing arts market has come to occupy a central place in the cycle of buying and selling live performance. Once, this commodification would have been anathema. Today, it is the norm. There are now arts markets throughout Asia, North and South America and the Pacific. Some events are huge and grotesque, others community occasions. Australia's are essentially booking services for those planning an overseas tour. But the question now is: has the arts market outlived its usefulness? Have the new digital platforms made touring redundant? Has the newly rapid, collaborative exchange of artistic practice made the whole idea unnecessary? Isn't the world simply saturated with contemporary dance, physical theatre and new music, not to say festivals and circuits? The Australian market, APAM, is seeking to reinvent itself away from its intensive four-day showcase to an elongated process. But reinvent to what? And where might it end?

AT YOUR LOCAL BOOSHOP FROM 1 NOVEMBER
AND AS A PAPERBACK OR ONLINE
FROM OUR WEBSITE AT
WWW.CURRENCYHOUSE.ORG.AU